THIS BOOK
BELONGS TO:

_____

Birth date:

_____

Birth time:

_____

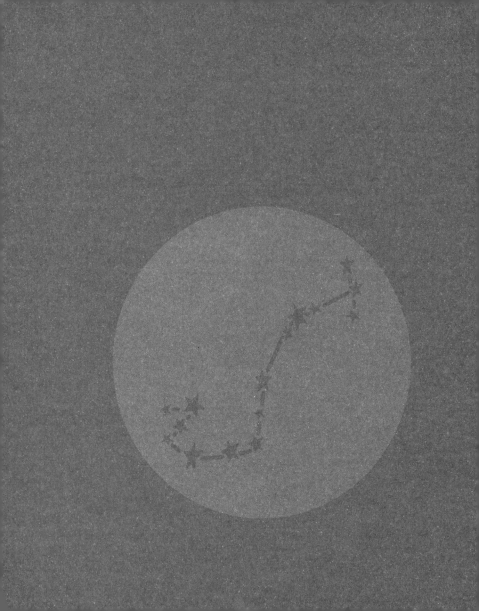

ZODIAC SIGNS

SCORPIO

ZODIAC SIGNS

SCORPIO

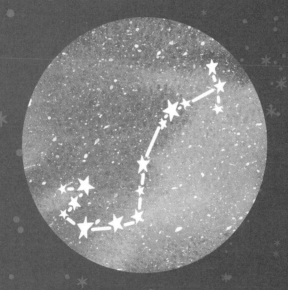

DANNY LARKIN

STERLING ETHOS
New York

STERLING ETHOS
New York

An Imprint of Sterling Publishing Co., Inc.
1166 Avenue of the Americas
New York, NY 10036

ISBN 978-1-4549-3898-9

Distributed in Canada by Sterling Publishing Co., Inc.
c/o Canadian Manda Group, 664 Annette Street
Toronto, Ontario M6S 2C8, Canada
Distributed in the United Kingdom by GMC Distribution Services
Castle Place, 166 High Street, Lewes, East Sussex BN7 1XU, England
Distributed in Australia by NewSouth Books
University of New South Wales, Sydney, NSW 2052, Australia

For information about custom editions, special sales, and premium
and corporate purchases, please contact Sterling Special Sales at
800-805-5489 or specialsales@sterlingpublishing.com.

Manufactured in China

2 4 6 8 10 9 7 5 3 1

sterlingpublishing.com

Cover design by Elizabeth Mihaltse Lindy
Cover and endpaper illustration by Sarah Frances
Interior design by Nancy Singer
Zodiac signs ©wikki33 and macrovector/freepik

CONTENTS

♏

INTRODUCTION

I began this book in Athens. I went to Greece in May 2019 to study the ancient mysteries of renewal and transformation with the astrologer Demetra George. She is truly a living legend. It was a mystical and transformative journey to several sacred ruins, concretizing the myths I've loved since I was a boy.

Astrology is an invitation into an ancient wisdom tradition. We all know that many people are born when the sun is in Scorpio, and that obviously they are different. This book is not going to try to prove the impossible—that somehow all Scorpios are the same. But it is the underlying principle of astrology that all Scorpios can become better versions of themselves by exploring the Scorpio symbols. And many Scorpios seem to resonate with these symbols and themes in such similar ways that we begin to see some common traits.

This book is first and foremost intended as a humorous

and accessible initiation into this set of symbols and how they manifest in different spheres and phases of life.

The constellation Scorpius, from which Scorpio is derived, is itself a potent and venomous creature with much to teach everyone who is born under its sign. Seriously, watch some scorpion footage on YouTube tonight if you want to deepen your intuitive grasp of this sun sign. The way scorpions strut about with a menacing stinger in plain sight of any creature that may try to cross it is a metaphor for how many Scorpios often seek to solve life's problems with intimidation and aggression. Whether most problems are solved or exacerbated by such strategies is an open question.

If you are a Scorpio, you were born in the middle of autumn, so fall symbols also speak deeply to you. Because the Scorpio season coincides with the middle of fall, it was considered a "solid" sign by ancient astrologers. In modern parlance, we call this a *fixed* sign. It is not the beginning or the end of the fall, in which the weather is more transitional, this is the time of the year when the weather is mostly fixed as fall. Mirroring their season, Scorpios prize staying power and consistency, but they can sometimes cling too stubbornly, which is an emotional dynamic that we will explore later in this book.

Scorpio is a water sign, so Scorpios will have a deep, powerful, lifelong relationship with water. And the mythological meanings of the Western esoteric tradition offer much food for thought for Scorpio, which we will explore in chapter two.

And finally, we will meet again and again with the two gods that rule Scorpio—Pluto and Mars. In ancient texts, Mars is the boss of any planet in Scorpio. After careful observation in the twentieth century, many modern astrologers now see the planet Pluto directing the flow of Scorpio energy. The myths of the gods after which these planets are named offer a wellspring of inspiration to Scorpios. These two gods will be explored in each chapter as relevant to the subject at hand.

After beginning this book in Greece, I finished it in the parks of New York City while gazing at turtles swimming in the pools of Central Park. As a water sign, Scorpio can gain clarity by being close to bodies of water and it's my hope that Scorpios will experience this gift often as they turn this book's pages.

SCORPIO

as a Child

I t's with a particular thrill that the Scorpio toddler discovers the word "No." It's good practice for any Scorpios
reading this book to pause right now and reflect on their
earliest memories of saying *no*. Perhaps these recollections
are similar to the moment when a baby scorpion first real-
izes its stinger has grown large enough to successfully hunt
and kill.

All children experience the terrible twos. However, each
sun sign progresses through this stage of development in a
profoundly different way. When Scorpio children discover
aggression, they are deeply intrigued and fascinated by the
apparent power they can wield over people. And of course,
they become frightened of the harm older and bigger adults
might inflict on them. They often become hyper-attuned to
both ends of the spectrum: how to hurt and how they might
be hurt. The anxiety that comes with this awareness means
they'll want to know early on how to defend themselves.
Other kids are more interested in toys; but threats, fighting,
and protection come early to many Scorpios.

Some Scorpio children might experience brutal trauma as children. Others might witness a friend or parent suffer a vicious attack—either physically, emotionally, mentally, or spiritually. Many Scorpios learn too soon how vicious this world can be. Other signs have their fair share of trauma, but for Scorpios it's especially meaningful. Bad things don't happen to people because they are Scorpios. But what differs between signs is the response to the trauma.

LEARNING TO FIGHT

Whereas other signs decide the solution is to check out into fantasy land (Pisces), or to try to be smarter than everyone else (Aquarius) or prettier than everyone else (Libra), or to work harder than everyone else (Capricorn), many Scorpios conclude as children that the way to stay safe is to fight more cunningly than everyone else. And this is why the ancient symbol of the scorpion is so potent. Just as scorpions meander with a massive stinger in plain view, many children decide the way to survive is to have the equivalent of a stinger: they want everyone to know that if you mess with them, it will hurt.

There are many ways to fight. A young Scorpio's fascination with the so-called art of war is shared with the sign Aries. Both are ruled by Mars, the Roman god of war whose planet is red. Aries fights in an overt, hot, and loud way, which befits a fire sign. Scorpio fights in more subtle ways, because it's a water sign. Many Scorpios discover early on the potency of the silent treatment or how to get what they want in more nuanced ways. Some Scorpios may not even be known as aggressive, fighting types. But truth be told, they excel at subtle hints, manipulation, and persuasion to get what they want. Subterfuge comes so naturally to these children. They sometimes giggle when they watch Aries try to shout someone down. *That's not how to get through to them, but I'm not going to tell you that,* young Scorpios tell themselves.

But many nuanced ways of fighting aren't yet possible for toddlers to comprehend. As the terrible twos unfold, Scorpio children may choose to manipulate the intensity and drama they can create by refusing to go along with what adults want done. Again, there's nothing a Scorpio toddler enjoys more than declaring "No!" and daring their parents to duke it out with them. They find their parents' psychological buttons and don't hesitate to push them when they don't get their way. Scorpio children have a way with one-liners that hit below the belt. Many parents learn to think twice before disappointing their Scorpio child, because they know all hell will break loose. The metaphorical stinger hangs above these kids. Some parents might grow to resent how their Scorpio children have the guts to call them on the stuff other kids and even adults might not have the courage to talk about. Other parents tire of the equivalent of psychological warfare when, for example, it's time for bed.

Some Scorpio children may be more subtle. This is always the million-dollar question about Scorpios: How open is their zest for a fight? Or how subtle and under-the-radar do they act? Some quickly adapt to their parents' styles and figure out how to get what they want without making a stink or fuss. It's amazing how quickly puppy-face gets some parents to melt into honoring their kids' wishes or relaxing some limit. But other Scorpio kids might pick the weirdest and most unexpected fights and throw tantrums when parents set reasonable limits that are actually keeping them safe and healthy.

For many Scorpios, it is a challenge throughout childhood to know which hill to die on when instigating conflict—which fights are worth picking and which will only exacerbate their frustrations. Young and unformed Scorpio children—like baby scorpions—are almost in awe of their potential ability to sting, and they reflexively attack too often. What they are too young to understand is that sometimes we, as adults, grapple with paradoxes that can't be successfully conquered through brute force. Scorpio kids can scream, fight, groan, curse, and attack with all their might, but when the dust settles, there are always some problems that still can't be resolved. And this frustrates the Scorpio child immensely—they'll be frustrated all their lives by the idea that some issues in life are like beasts immune to their stingers' poison. And they are often too young to understand a paradox when they see one.

Scorpio children might delude themselves into thinking they can force a solution to any problem they face. They can be incredibly persuasive and perceptive, and they know it. But this talent can also backfire into an inferiority complex. These children may despise themselves for not being able to resolve some impossible Herculean problem. They are too young to understand that some problems can't be solved. It's helpful for parents to remind their Scorpio kids that they don't have to be superheroes to be special. Some problems are beyond the powers of both parent and child to fix. This is a bitter pill to swallow. But scorpions can't swim, and they can't fight an octopus. Learning to accept limits is key here.

PLAYING IN THE WATER

Scorpio is a water sign. Fighting with water is a potent metaphor for these children to unpack and explore. Parents should seriously consider buying their Scorpio kids a powerful water gun so that they can play out this symbolism in a fun way during the summer. Water parks are another winning summer activity. It will bring Scorpio children immense joy to splash their friends and family—letting go of some of that aggression in a playful, non-harmful way.

Another clever way to galvanize a Scorpio child's development as a water sign is to take them to the aquarium. Underwater predators will fascinate these kids. They will love learning about all the ways the creatures of the sea protect themselves and hunt. Squids shoot ink. Electric eels shock. Jellyfish sting. Octopuses strangle. But equally important for them to learn about is how some fish evade instead of fighting. There are some very fast swimmers that simply outrun the sharks. These kids—and many Scorpio adults for that matter—would benefit from seeing how sometimes winning means *not* fighting. Sometimes the aquatic creature wins by not fighting, escaping danger for a nicer part of the sea with tasty food where it can just chill.

In nature, water has a way of seeking out the lowest possible ground. And part of the watery quality of Scorpio is a lifelong relationship with depth. Many little scorpions have far deeper and more mysterious thoughts than their peers. It can almost take parents aback, the way their young kids ask deep, emotional, probing questions about the human condition at such an early age. They are old souls in this way. It's crucial for parents to be prepared to answer the hard questions in age-appropriate ways. Little scorpions can push to learn and try to understand things that they may actually not be old enough or emotionally ready to integrate. And this frustrates them to no end. It's crucial for parents to seek guidance and counsel about how and when to answer these questions in ways that are honest but also appropriate for kids.

Parents need to be incredibly mindful of discretion. Scorpio children might eavesdrop on their parents' conversations, later weaponizing what they've overheard. It can be a bit surprising, what comes out of a Scorpio child's mouth, and what they remember, or what they caught wind of one night when you thought they were sleeping.

Parenting a Scorpio child is not for the faint of heart. It requires iron tolerance and forbearance, particularly when baby Scorpios overreact to things that ultimately don't matter. These children are quick to retaliate, hit below the belt, play mind games, and push buttons, and often there's no reason for the fuss. Little Scorpios aren't old enough yet to know the wisdom of sparing themselves the pain of making mountains out of molehills. They must learn the hard way to pick their battles, and when the strongest thing they can do is to let it go. Why freak out and panic and lose the day to something that doesn't really matter? Or, as Cher puts in her own special way in capital letters on her Twitter Bio page, "DOESNT MATTER in 5 yrs IT DOESNT MATTER THERE'S ONLY LOVE&FEAR." Hopefully, Scorpio children can come to this realization before they are as old as Cher.

Scorpio is ruled by two different planets in astrology. When the sun shines in the sign of Scorpio, these ruling planets are like celestial bosses that order the sun around and tell it how to shine its light. In ancient astrology, the war god's planet Mars rules Scorpio. This augurs how Scorpios can be quick to believe that the only way to get what they want is to wage war against someone else.

However, in modern astrology, Scorpio is ruled and ordered around by the remote planet Pluto. This dwarf planet's discovery corresponds with the atom bomb as well as the emergence and popularization of psychology. And in many young Scorpios, there is a tendency both to go nuclear and to try to engage in intense psychological warfare. What these kids don't always get is that sometimes a subtle, polite request works better.

Many parents struggle to persuade their Scorpio children that gentler and softer ways may be better in terms of achieving their agendas. But it is the recurring perception of Scorpios in both childhood and adulthood that the only way to win is to fight dirty, leverage secrets, and get inside other people's heads—to frighten and to raise hell. What many Scorpios fail to see is that they often up the ante with a mean comment or a probing question. This perception of a world that feels out to get them is actually, in truth, a series of retaliations for when Scorpio crossed the line, and other people pushed back. "You didn't need to get that nasty" is a piece of feedback Scorpio kids often receive, but struggle to heed and integrate.

LEARNING TO DISGUISE

Halloween fascinates Scorpio children. Many of them have significant experiences in Halloween costumes. Of course, the sun is in Scorpio on October 31. The Scorpio child appreciates the theatrical opportunity to portray a mythological character and explore the more gruesome themes it may represent. It's amazing how Halloween is often the first conduit for children to learn about death, magic, and the occult. But just as importantly, the young Scorpio is fascinated by the costumes that other children select. The costume selections of their friends and family can be quite revealing of inner psychological issues. Ruled by Pluto, many young Scorpios have a knack for psychology, for picking up on the subtle nuances of personality that other people might miss. And so when Halloween comes around, they often can see the deeper meanings in why certain classmates picked certain outfits.

Discussing Halloween costumes is an excellent way for parents to explore psychology in a developmentally appropriate way with their Scorpio child, although it may be surprising for parents to hear what their child reveals. For Scorpios reading this book, it may well be useful to pause for a moment and recall some of your most significant childhood memories of becoming something else and transforming on Halloween.

In addition to Halloween, Scorpio children connect energetically with autumn. The sun is in the sign of Scorpio between October 23 and November 21, though dates may differ from year to year. It's the time of year when the leaves turn crimson and yellow and all the plants begin to die.

Autumn festivals create a safe container for Scorpios to understand nature's cycle of life which resonates with them deeply.

HADES AND PERSEPHONE

Pondering the Ancient Greek myth that explains the first fall, and the cycle of seasons, can give us some further insights into the intense experiences that Scorpios have as children. Here's the condensed version: Earth was once always bountiful and perpetually in harvest. This abundance was presided over by Demeter, the goddess of agriculture. Demeter had a daughter, Persephone. One day, Persephone wandered away from her mother and picked the powerful and aromatic narcissus flower. Upon plucking the flower, the ground beneath her opened up and out sprang Hades, the lord of the underworld, in a chariot pulled by his dark horses. He abducted Persephone, put her in his chariot, took her down to the underworld, stole her virginity, and made her his bride and queen.

Poor Demeter didn't know where Persephone had gone. She searched and searched but couldn't find her daughter anywhere on earth. Finally, she talked with the sun god Helios, who could see everything, and he revealed to her that Hades had taken Persephone to the underworld. She then went straight to the king of the gods, her brother Zeus, and told him to order Hades to return her daughter. She was dismayed to discover that Zeus actually approved of Hades and Persephone marrying and wasn't going to interfere. In Greek mythology, an uncle and niece marrying in the family of gods wasn't a big deal. But Demeter was livid because her brothers hadn't consulted her.

Demeter retaliated against Zeus and Hades for scheming to take away her daughter by inflicting a massive famine upon the earth. The eternal spring ended, and the first fall and winter descended upon the earth. Human beings began to suffer and die from starvation. Zeus soon realized that all humans would die, which consequently meant no one would make offerings to him or honor him. And so out of vanity and so that he would continue to be honored, he sought to find a way to make peace with his sister and brother over Persephone's fate. That way, humans would continue to live, prosper, and worship him.

A truce was negotiated so that Persephone would spend six months of the year on the earth with her mother, Demeter, and six months of the year with her husband, Hades. Originally, Demeter had hoped that the marriage could be annulled and that Persephone could return to the earth full-time. However, once humans died and ate the food of the underworld, they entered into Hades' jurisdiction. The same was true for Persephone, who had eaten six pomegranate arils while underground. Therefore, Hades insisted she had to spend some time there. This compromise was agreed upon by all the gods. But, to keep score and to get back at her brothers, Demeter decided that when Persephone was gone from her side and with Hades, it would be autumn and winter. And when Persephone came back to her side, the earth would become fruitful again, and it would be spring and summer.

This is one of the most intense and powerful stories in Greek mythology, and it holds some keys to unlocking Scorpios' childhoods. Many Scorpios, no matter where they fall on the gender spectrum, have experiences that allow them to identify strongly with Persephone's loss of innocence.

So often there is a ripping away of the naïvety of childhood. Many take a journey into the underworld that leaves them forever changed. But they also grow up too soon, and the feeling of having innocence ripped away can be very painful.

There is also a push and pull between Scorpio children and their mother, which can be compared to the Persephone–Demeter dynamic. Like all children, there is a yearning to be close and get the special chemical releases in the brain that only mother can unlock. But there is also a conflicting desire to pull away and discover the corners of the world that mother would fear our visiting. Of course, mother's fear of these places is what makes them irresistibly intriguing to explore. This makes for some theatrical episodes of teenage rebellion. But some Scorpios struggle to outgrow this dynamic. As they step into maturity, it will be a major test whether they spend their adult lives trying to prove a point to their moms, or if they focus instead on becoming their authentic selves—regardless of the responses their choices would provoke.

SCORPIO

as an Adult

As adults, Scorpios keep getting the same feedback: *You are too intense*. But the meaning of the phrase rarely registers. They just don't get it.

"Why are you saying 'too intense' like it's a bad thing?" a Scorpio wonders.

"And plus, I was actually holding back," a Scorpio tells herself, patting herself on the back.

So what was supposed to be criticism ends up being taken as a compliment. The reaction their intensity tends to provoke actually reads as success to Scorpios—they see an offended person as someone they have successfully gotten through to. Is it really Scorpios' problem that other people can't handle the bitter truth?

What does "intense" really mean, anyway? Is intensity like beauty: in the eye of the beholder? Yes and no. It behooves all Scorpio adults to ponder the etymology of this word "intense," which is so often thrown at them. The English took the word from the French. And to be in Paris, where criticizing others is a kind of high art, gives you a taste of the French usage of this word. Scorpio adults, like the French often are, can be hard on other people, and will sting like a scorpion when they see something that needs to be corrected.

But we can glean more insights, moving beyond the quirks of French culture, when we look back at the Latin roots of the French word: *intentus* and *intensus*. These are the roots of "intent" and "intense," and they are closely linked. Both spring from the older Latin root: *tensus*. This root word *tensus* means to stretch and strain. And this meaning is still salient in our modern English word "tension." But whereas *tensus* in Latin is a physical tension, *intentus* and *intensus* developed as variants to express a kind of mental pull. This etymological bond reflects how a major aspect of intensity is a clear and strong intention to make a stretch toward a certain goal dominate the moment.

Often there is an agenda and an intention that Scorpios are trying to enact. Now, in a Scorpio's mind, everyone has an agenda and intention like Scorpios do all the time. It seems foreign to them that people sometimes might just want to let their hair down and relax. And it seems like a ruse: there must be something hidden. In fact, the more the moment is about "chillaxing," the more Scorpio's spidey sense gets tripped up and the more suspicious they grow of everyone else's hidden agenda. And a lot of Scorpios' problems as adults seem to start when they fall out of alignment with their partner, friends, family, or colleagues who just want to chill for a moment. Meanwhile, Scorpio goes against the moment with their *Intentions* with a capital I, deciding that now is the time. And everyone else is like, "Actually, now is *not* the time, we are all trying to relax here." And Scorpio is like, "Liars—no one is ever *just* relaxing." And everyone else responds: ". . . you need to relax."

There is one more insight about intensity that we can glean from the old utterances of the Roman Empire, by expanding on the idea of stretching inherent in *tensus*. There is an eagerness in Scorpio to stretch and push forward with intention against any resistance. In this sense, it can be revealing to think about the variant spelling of intention as "intension." Sticking with an intention often puts us into a state of tension, and intensity sometimes results in enforcing an intention and insisting on a mental and emotional stretch.

Scorpios, as adults, get frustrated with most human beings. When they look at their partners, their friends, their colleagues, and their families, they keep seeing the same thing: people who could be pushing themselves more but aren't. Scorpios don't perceive such mediocrity from the position of the lazy armchair critic—they observe as people who have challenged themselves very hard to become better versions of themselves. It's almost like Scorpios want to scream at everyone: "I walked to school barefoot in the winter through six inches of snow, and so can you. I walked over coals barefoot, and so can you!" But actually, what most Scorpios don't fully understand is that they possess a unique gift to be able to tolerate a higher level of mental and emotional anguish than most other individuals which helps them manifest an intention they prize.

Scorpios have a potent relationship with the vow. They make these powerful promises to themselves and others, and they stick to them with tenacity. To fully understand this resonance, it would be helpful to dive into some of the water mythology that underlies astrology.

In modern times, many astrologers see the planet Pluto as the ruler of Scorpio. This means that the King of the Underworld, known as Pluto to the Romans and Hades to the Greeks, is like the boss of the sun to Scorpios. In astrological doctrine, Pluto orders the sun around and tells it how to shine. The sun corresponds to the mind, soul, and judgment of the individual. Thus, the god Hades energetically commands the mind and soul. Deep within the psyche of Scorpios, there is an unconscious drive to honor Hades and to connect with underworld energies to enact agendas and achieve goals. Now, at first, this might sound a little silly. Most Scorpios don't fancy themselves Neo-pagans who yearn to make offerings to an old Pagan god of the subterranean realm of the dead, or pause for a moment to wonder "What would Pluto do?". What rulership really means is that Scorpios are more attuned to the psychological forces that Ancient Greeks associated with Hades and his realm of the underworld. And by exploring some of the mythological stories associated with Hades, Scorpios can gain keys to how to unlock their own inner doors and become better versions of themselves.

Scorpios are not all carbon copies of one another. But the premise of astrology is that there is something in these symbols and stories that will fire Scorpios' imaginations more profoundly than other signs, and will galvanize their individuation, to use the term C. G. Jung coined to express embracing the unique process it takes to fully become our singular selves.

RIVERS OF THE UNDERWORLD

The ancient Greek underworld was completely different from the Christian conception of hell. And so we need to begin by disentangling the two. Dante Alighieri was an incredible writer who mixed Christian and Pagan elements to create a fascinating piece of literature about hell, purgatory, and paradise. His *Divine Comedy* (1320) is one of the great masterpieces of late Medieval literature. However, the collateral damage of his explosive popularity is that we often project Dante onto our mental images of the underworld. And, truth be told, a different underworld emerges when we go to the older texts of the Greeks and Romans. The fire of Medieval hell is nowhere to be found; instead, we meet a cooler watery realm with numerous rivers flowing through it. These rivers each possessed a magical power.

Scorpio is a water sign. As Scorpios move through adulthood, the symbolism of these underworld rivers can help us understand the potency they bring to every interaction. To compare signs, Scorpio wades through water in a profoundly different way than Cancer or Pisces, which are the other two water signs of the zodiac. It is this underworld element that differentiates them. There is something darker and more mysterious about how Scorpio travels through the world. These rivers that the ancients perceived to be flowing deep underneath the earth in the underworld tell us much about what lies in the emotional depths of many Scorpios.

Before continuing with our exploration of this line of thinking, I wish to acknowledge Liz Greene. She is one of the most influential astrologers of the twentieth and twenty-first centuries. She pioneered a new synthesis of astrology and depth psychology with Howard Sasportas. We lost Howard too soon to AIDS. Liz Greene's exploration of underworld rivers forms one strand of her influential work on Pluto. I traveled to Cornwall in England to study with Liz in person in 2017. I also participated in her online Pluto seminars in 2016. Liz outlined this approach to Pluto in her book *The Astrology of Fate* (1984), which is a dense but excellent read. It is hard to say that astrological doctrines and ideas belong to any single person. But I do wish to acknowledge the tremendous inspiration I have drawn from Liz Greene which informs the following accessible primer on how the rivers of the underworld flow and ripple through Scorpios' minds.

Acheron

And so we begin, as the old stories often did, with the river Acheron, which means "River of Woe." Now, that not might sound very uplifting; but let's face it, many Scorpios battle with intense feelings of melancholia as adults. And as astrologers, we want to inspire and teach Scorpios how to better handle this river within and transmute this melancholia that often hangs over them like a dark cloud.

In ancient Greece, when a person died, the living relatives left a coin under the dead person's tongue. The deceased would then use this coin to pay Charon, the ferryman, who would take the newly dead across the river Acheron to the underworld. So the Acheron was the first river of the underworld that newly dead souls would encounter. Many Scorpios have powerful experiences with death. Some have near-death experiences. Other Scorpios are called upon to serve the dying. Other Scorpios are deeply touched by the death of a parent, family member, or friend.

This is a hard point to explore, because death touches all of us. All of us must bear the weight articulated so pithily by that old Latin aphorism *Ars longa, Vita brevis*. Art is long, Life is brief. But different sun signs experience the inevitability of death and its ever-present specter in profoundly different ways. Most signs just shut down. Gemini tells a funny story but buries its feelings. Aries avoids it and finds something else that doesn't actually matter to be angry about and yells and screams. Pisces drinks its feelings away or finds another way to escape. But Scorpio seems more receptive to death and to the deep and the rewarding, albeit frightening, insights that can come from contemplating the brevity of life. In this there is melancholia, but there is also much richness.

But from this awareness also stems much of the way Scorpio resents others. Don't these people realize how short life is? Why are they wasting their time "under-being"? Who knows how long they have? Such morbid thoughts are mostly thought by Scorpio but often held in and left unexpressed. Finding a healthy outlet for these stirrings is of utmost importance. I hate how the standard advice for Scorpios is to seek out therapy. All signs benefit from exploring their own psyches more. However, what many Scorpios really need is a friend they can "go there" with—a friend who can go to the underworld with them and talk about the dirty, scary, frightening truths that bubble beneath the surface but that Scorpios fear being open about.

Scorpios can feel an incredible attraction toward stepping into the role of Charon. They may feel a yearning to care for other souls. But the key is to balance this motivation with their own inner work. Only a divine being could ferry the dead in perpetuity. The rest of us mere mortals need a break. Some Scorpios might arrogantly think they can be Charon, overburdening themselves with relationships in which they are the caretaker of someone else's deepest, darkest secrets. It will be a lifelong challenge to understand how to balance their talent for this role with other aspects of their lives.

Styx

Let's move on to the next river, the Styx. Styx is an intriguing chthonic deity whose story is seldom told. Styx was originally a water nymph. She was one of many sisters, who were collectively known as the Oceanides. Styx was the daughter of Titan Okeanos, the original ruler of the sea before the Titans were defeated and the sea was given to Poseidon. Now Styx was actually present at the abduction of Persephone by Hades; she was one of the nymphs attending to her. But Styx's story does not end here. During the epic war between Zeus and Saturn and their respective allies, Zeus called all immortals to Mount Olympus and promised any deity that took his side enduring power and respect if they swore an oath to him. Most Titans sided with Saturn and lost. But upon the advice of her father, Styx bucked the trend and came with her children to pledge loyalty to Zeus. Her children were quite powerful—Nike (victory), Zelus (rivalry), Cratus (strength), and Bia (Force), and they helped Zeus win.

Zeus elevated Styx into the powerful underworld river of oaths. Oaths would be sworn upon her—by both mortals and immortals—and if you broke your oath, you would incur her wrath. In ancient art, we see images of Iris, the rainbow messenger goddess, who would bring a jug of water from the Styx in the underworld to the gods on Mount Olympus for them to use to make promises, which the Styx would then enforce.

The oath is a potent and sacred concept for many Scorpios. Everyone makes promises. And many of us break promises to others and to ourselves. And while many of us seem to have accepted long ago that this is part and parcel of this comedy of errors known as the human condition, many Scorpios can't get on board with this. There is something deep within many Scorpios that cries out to honor the Styx and the sanctity of certain vows. And Scorpios may well have a point. Recovering alcoholics take a vow to never drink again and count their days of sobriety. Sticking to that vow is the bedrock foundation of that program of recovery. There is great wisdom here that healing entails drawing certain red lines that we never cross again no matter what. Those of us who aren't alcoholics may well suffer from other destructive compulsive behaviors. And we may benefit from discerning and respecting certain bottom lines. This process comes easier to Scorpios than to other signs. So Scorpios often find themselves in the position of the Styx, holding people accountable to the importance of keeping a promise—but also staring at the world in bewilderment as a diet gets broken yet again, or a gym membership goes unused, or agreements struck at an annual performance review go unimplemented. Scorpios are sometimes accused of being angry. But when they work so hard at holding themselves to certain vows, it can become enraging when others don't.

The Styx was also the river that Thetis dipped her son Achilles in to make him nearly invincible—save for the notorious heel by which she dangled him. Scorpios need to be very careful of falling into the delusion that they are invincible, because everyone has an Achilles heel. Most Scorpios don't think they are literally invincible. But driven as they are to stick to their vows, they can become self-righteous as they watch other people stumble as they stay the course. But while Scorpios may stay the course on many things, they can't remain completely consistent on *all* things. They have their own places where they stumble again and again. In this way, some Scorpios may have a fundamental weakness that they are incredibly ashamed about and which they seek to hide. The problem with this concealment and Scorpio's desire to avoid talking about it is that they often deny themselves the emotional support that they need the most.

Lethe

Next, let's look at the river Lethe. Lethe was the river of forgetfulness, concealment, and oblivion. Souls would drink from this river to forget their past lives and prepare to return to earth in a new incarnation. It was also understood to be the river of letting go. Within each Scorpio there is a latent ability to master the art of letting go. But while many of us can appreciate the letting go as an ideal, we struggle to release anguish and pain about the past in practice. It is easier said than done. Carl Jung comes to mind with an insight about how to get better at letting go. Jung once said, "I am not what happened to me . . . I am what I choose to become." It's intriguing how Jung connects letting go with ushering in a new future, just as in ancient mythology the purpose of the Lethe waters was letting go in order to prepare for a new life.

In Scorpios, there is an avid hunger to better understand the process of letting go and to transform. It can lead them to various occult, spiritual, and psychological interests that deepen the soul. But all this knowledge can backfire. Scorpios can appoint themselves other people's shamans, convinced they can use all their knowledge to force an issue with someone. But they do so at their own peril. And they may need to hold back on their desire to tell someone to get over it already or get off their pity pot and get to work. If only shaming people really worked. It would do well for Scorpios to remember the fall season into which they were born. It would be silly to expect the leaves of an autumn tree to turn yellow, orange, or crimson in August. Just as you can't force a tree to prematurely let go of its leaves, we can't force humans to go against their own wishes or speed up their inner processes. Scorpios can delude themselves into thinking their "Jedi mind tricks" are causing someone to change faster. But often the person is just telling lies to appease the scorpion in their lives. What Scorpios really need to do is focus more on the things *they* are struggling to let go of and to get to work on envisioning and imagining what they actually want to be, and on supporting other people in what they wish to become in their own terms, ways, and time.

This Lethe energy is one of the greatest blessings for Scorpios in the unique way they experience Scorpio as a water sign. If properly understood, the Lethe's flow can be channeled into healing and releasing the deepest emotional challenges that face Scorpios. The overuse of the word "transformation" has emptied it of most of its meaning. In the esoteric tradition, we revere the ancient stories of the underworld journey as an archetype for the transformation and healing we seek here on earth. The deep wisdom within many Scorpios is an appreciation for the patience it takes to go on an underworld journey to reach the Lethe. Just as the Lethe was not the first river shore that souls encountered, Scorpios show that tenacity is toughing out the required journey along the Acheron first. So often, implementing a new pattern requires a period of difficult adjustment that can cause some of us to break under emotional pressure and revert back to the undesired pattern. Scorpios can stick with it even when it gets tough, and they won't give up too soon. "Don't quit five minutes before the miracle" is advice this sign should keep in mind. This tenacity means that Scorpios might be more successful at transformation than other signs.

Cocytus and Phlegethon

Two other underworld rivers we also see mentioned in ancient sources are the river of wailing—the Cocytus—and the river of fire, the Phlegethon. It is ironic that the Christian imagination became stuck on the fire of the Phlegethon and the wailing conveyed by the Cocytus. In ancient mythology, the Acheron, the Styx, and the Lethe had more stories of interacting with both gods and humans. But the insight here is that many Scorpios struggle with intense anguish that burns inside of them. Or they can turn on the people close to them when they miss the mark and unleash rivers of fire and wailing. Everyone makes mistakes, and whether fire and brimstone works to resolve this is dubious. Part of the work for Scorpios, ruled by Mars and Pluto, is to understand how to hold their fire, lest they burn bridges among friends, family, and colleagues.

Scorpios have a lifelong relationship with the symbols and rivers of the underworld as adults. When Carl Jung coined individuation, his point was that each adult goes on a journey to discover symbols that speak to their subconscious which galvanizes their inner healing. This section—

Scorpio as an Adult—has been intended as an introduction to the rich symbols of the underworld. They are like keys. With further work and exploration of these themes, Scorpios can glean the insights into the underworld transformation they are craving.

SCORPIO

as a Parent

et's start with a deceptively basic fact: it is very likely that when a Scorpio adult starts parenting, their child will not be a Scorpio. Early on in this journey of raising kids, as the child's personality beings to sparkle, Scorpios may discover their daughter or son is not as intense or deep as they are. And it's probably for the better . . . because let's face it, Scorpio kids can be tough to handle. And two Scorpios under one roof is a lot for everyone else in the family. But for the vast majority of Scorpio parents reading this, it's important to start by reflecting on what it might mean that parent and child have different sun signs.

UNDERSTANDING A CHILD'S UNIQUE NEEDS

As parenting unfolds, we can get sidetracked trying to give our children what we wish we had gotten. At first, this seems like a totally valid proposition. And it can feel so gratifying to break family patterns and give our kids what we never received. But what if your kids need something entirely different than what you needed? Yes, we all need food and shelter. If only emotional needs were that simple. What gets particularly tricky is that sometimes it's hard to tell what a kid needs. Sometimes children don't know how they feel, or are struggling to put words to psychodynamics they aren't old enough to understand. And in those situations, it seems natural to reach back into the reservoirs of our own experiences and fill in the blanks with our own stories. But that's actually where the trouble starts.

One paradox of family life is that we are simultaneously so similar and so different. The genes we share with our biological children can at times lead us to feel like we have a lot in common with them. And our kids may well have certain physical and emotional traits that run in the family. But that's not the full story. The Western esoteric tradition posits that on a spiritual level, each child has their own unique soul, their own unique mind, and their own special spark of the divine that ignites an inner fire like no one else's.

In this way, astrology can be a revealing way to start to explore and understand the uniqueness growing and

SCORPIO

unfolding inside our kids. As astrologers, we analyze the sky at the moment of birth. The positions of the sun, moon, and planets stand as omens for the child's unique destiny as they become who they are meant to be. And there will be an invitation throughout the parenting process to honor your child's gifts and to think about how to nurture them to become the best version of themselves. Many parents find it useful to consult with a professional astrologer for perspective on how better to understand the esoteric symbols that might speak to their child's development.

TEACHING CHILDREN

Scorpios can make wonderful parents. As water signs, they can become attuned to the emotional needs of their child with a depth that few other signs can match. But the key challenge for them is honoring how their child learns and receives emotional insights. And Scorpios will need to monitor their intensity levels. What, when, and how they teach their kids how the world actually works matters. They must take special care not to overwhelm their children. Just because a child asks questions and says they are ready for the answer doesn't mean they actually are. Scorpios will also need to carefully deliberate when to hold back and be silent and to let their kids learn something on their own. Or when to wait until a future opportunity when they are older and mature enough to share an insight.

Sometimes kids need to come home and get a big hug after they royally mess up, especially when they own up to it without playing games. This may be difficult for Scorpio parents, because when children make errors, their knee-jerk reaction may well be that a sting is in order to teach them a lesson they won't forget. But sometimes tenderness and compassion will help a child to integrate a mistake's lesson more than a severe or punitive response. Instigating a shame spiral isn't ultimately that constructive for the child. First, it makes them scared to be open and honest again. Second, shame is actually not a nuanced emotion, it's just terribly unpleasant. And what most child psychologists talk about is getting children into a more reflective and analytical space.

Most kids aspire to be successful, effective, and affable. Often, when kids make mistakes and miss the mark, it's

SCORPIO

because something came up that prevented them from succeeding. There is often something physically, emotionally, or socially uncomfortable that they haven't integrated, and they've cracked under the pressure. What most kids need to do after they mess up is to pause and think hard. What is a different way they could have handled this? Is there a different coping strategy that perhaps they could have tried out? As a parent, your role is to help facilitate reflection. There is a way to lovingly explore a difficult mistake so that the child feels loved but also inspired to try again tomorrow in a different and smarter way. Shame shuts down this process.

There is an old British proverb that most Scorpios resent: you catch more flies with honey than with vinegar. Most Scorpios think the real solution to catching flies is to get an industrial-strength bug zapper. But teaching children to become better versions of themselves is a far more complex undertaking than killing bugs. Very often, there is a bitter pill that kids need to swallow, and a bit of sweetness goes a long way. Perhaps, since military metaphors speak more cogently to Scorpio's psyche than an antiquated honey analogy, we can explore this more with militaristic symbolism. Your kid is going off to war the next morning when they leave for school. Try to think of preparing your kid for battle. Feed them the best food, make them laugh, help them to relax so they can sleep like a baby. And slip in one gentle insight in response to what they've shared about the anxieties and frustrations of their day. They will then arise in the morning well rested and ready to take the playground by storm.

Scorpio parents badly want to nurture their child by sharing deep insights with them. It's almost like the logic of an emotional vaccine. It is a noble intention to make their childhood easier. *Kid, take it from me, you don't want to learn things the hard way.* But Scorpio parents have a way of making dinner conversations or rides in the car way more intense than they need to. Sometimes people are starving, and it's not really the time to have a big talk after just a few bites of food. Sometimes it's been a long day and people are too tired to zoom out and think big-picture. But Scorpio parents can't help themselves, and they pour their heart and soul into a long meandering monologue that unfortunately goes in one ear and out the other. If the kid isn't interested, Scorpios nevertheless tell themselves that some of it is *probably* getting through and sticking.

Or the parent decides the kid *should* be interested and it's the right thing to force them to put up with a lecture that they are just going to tune out. Some kids of Scorpio parents just want to giggle with their families and tell some funny stories after a long day at school. But the Scorpio parent keeps wanting to go there and get really intense at the dinner table. In all these cases, the Scorpio parent is deluding themselves. Timing is everything. And it's crucial throughout the parenting process to attune to when the child will be receptive to hearing a deeper insight. As a water sign, the Scorpio parent has much to teach their child about resilience. Each of us has a well inside us that we can draw water from when times get tough. It would be a shame for the kid to miss out on these insights. Sometimes, a Scorpio needs to hold a thought and wait for a more opportune time to share.

Nothing makes a Scorpio parent happier than when their child asks one of the big questions. Just try and remember to share *one* age-appropriate insight, not twelve. Share insights in small chunks and gauge how the kid is absorbing and metabolizing the material. Sometimes the poor kids of Scorpios get more than they bargained for and don't know how to break it to their parents that they have no idea what their mom or dad is talking about anymore.

DISCIPLINING CHILDREN

Scorpio parents need to monitor their relationship with punishing their kids. Children make mistakes on the road to development. Kids test the moral limits they are still learning. As they grow into teenagers, rebellion can become very seductive. Because Scorpio parents often have fixed ideas about right and wrong, can be very opinionated about them, and can express themselves quite harshly, this makes rebelling against them particularly alluring to children. Scorpios need to guard against creating a negative feedback loop in which their harsh responses to rebellious behavior only end up encouraging the teenager to try and get a rise out of mom or dad again. Scorpios may benefit from exploring different models of punishment and reward with a psychotherapist or a trusted friend. There are many ways to respond to an episode when a child or teenager crosses a red line. And there are particular strategies that Scorpios can explore to defuse and discourage provocation.

Scorpio parents worry too much about their kids when they are away from home and out of their sight. While it is natural and healthy for all parents to fret about their child's safety, Scorpios may exaggerate the threat levels and perceive dangers that aren't happening. This is where the energy of Pluto as the ruler of Scorpio and the flow of the underworld rivers can present a challenge. Scorpios know how screwed up this world can be and fear their child will be harmed when they aren't there to protect them. What's more important than wailing at and fearing the river Cocytus is actually teaching their kids how to be street-smart and observant. Instead of holding these powerful feelings of fear inside, work with your co-parent and your friends to come up with creative ways to inspire your children to be clever when they are on their own.

CONNECTING WITH CHILDREN

It's good for Scorpios to enjoy the fall season with their kids. But please, push this further than getting a pumpkin spice latte. Go apple-picking if you live near orchards. Make apple cider from scratch. Take the children to the farmer's market and cook them fresh food that is only available during the autumn. Check out the changing leaves if they are nearby, and revel in the waves of crimson, gold, and orange. Go pumpkin-picking and carve out jack-o'-lanterns at home. It may be messy, but it's worth it. Splurge on Halloween costumes for the kids and allow them to explore their curiosities. There is a way that all Scorpios become so excited when it is the middle of fall and the sun has returned to the sign of Scorpio. Earlier on in this chapter, the advice was given to wait for the opportune time. There is a way that diving into the rituals of fall and the turning of the seasons will create an opening for connection with your children. They may become more receptive to an insight you have long wanted to share about the meaning of life. It is good for children to study nature and to witness how we reap and sow at harvest time. Sometimes showing is more powerful than telling.

SCORPIO

in Love

With Scorpios, it always starts with that intense look in the eyes. They're immediately drawn to any person who can meet and match their piercing gaze. They find it very alluring when someone can flash an amorous look that speaks words the tongue cannot utter. And Scorpios may well make a beeline across an entire room at a party to open a conversation if someone's gaze feels strong, deep, and intense enough. When glancing at online profile photos, they feel a similar thrill when there is something (even if it's Photoshopped) about the eyes. Scorpios are such suckers for eyes that they may not even care that the sparkle they see is actually a Snapchat filter.

The trouble for Scorpios can start as soon as they open their mouth to begin a conversation with the individual who has caught their eye. Flirting is supposed to be light, carefree, easy, and fun. But Scorpios like substance, shattering insights, darkness, and secrecy. They feel irresistibly drawn toward redirecting the conversation from small talk to deep talk. "Oh, wow, you want to take the conversation there," the targets of Scorpio's advances often remark to themselves. It seems lost on Scorpio that speaking lightly with an "I want to have sex and love you for the rest of my life" look in their eyes is intense and charged enough.

Scorpios need to work on not getting carried away into darker and weirder topics. That tendency is why so many Scorpios get turned down for a second date. In this sense, Scorpios might benefit from having a best friend with whom they can explore all this material that fascinates them. When it comes to the opening moves with a new potential lover, they will have an easier time holding back and not overwhelming their sweetheart, knowing they can just text their best friend with that weird thought instead.

SCORPIO IN LOVE

When Scorpios become infatuated, it can be hard for them to distinguish whether something is first-date or tenth-date material. They're prone to thinking a date's curiosity and admiration is carte blanche to hold a microphone to their internal monologue and share everything. Scorpios may think they know this, but in the heat of the moment, they're prone to excitedly overshare. It's not that certain topics like politics, sex, religion, or our pasts (and all of our exes) are off limits on early dates; it's just that it may be better for developing relationships if we tread carefully. Scorpio's way of broaching these topics—that is, with way too much intensity and detail—is problematic. Perhaps it's analogous to light levels. A light in darkness is desirable, but don't shine it so brightly that it blinds the other person.

Let's bring this down to the practical level. When someone vents about the sad state of politics on a date, the right move is generally to make a light-hearted joke and then listen to the response to see how much that person really wants to talk about it. Were they just venting for a moment or do they want to dive into this subject? Their response will tell you how to steer the conversation going forward. When someone brings up an ex, the key is to validate their feelings but not to draw the discussion out or ask a lot of follow-up questions, and then perhaps crack a joke to pivot to something lighter. Successful dating escalates intensity mutually, with conversation partners embracing their roles as copilots.

Scorpios can be so enthusiastic with what they want to share that they forget to check the temperature when a new topic comes up. A long diatribe sharing numerous insights without pause might well be one of Scorpio's most irritating traits early on in dating. The poor person across the table might feel like they just opened up Pandora's box. If the topic is intellectual, they might feel condescended to, because half the things Scorpio lectures them about, they already know. It can get too professorial, as over-enthused Scorpio tries to get to the bottom of things and reveal the ultimate truth that the other person didn't even ask for. If the topic is emotional, the other person can quickly get overwhelmed. "I actually wasn't really ready to talk about this heavy stuff with you yet, because I am still getting to know you," the dates say to themselves. They conclude that Scorpio sucks at reading them and feel uneasy. Scorpio thinks they are doing this person a favor by enlightening them, but are actually just turning the other person off.

Scorpios might also need to work on keeping their love of psychology in check. As the date unfolds, the apple of their eye is going to drop hints and reveal certain parts of their story. Scorpios will get to work on trying to figure them out. Don't jump to premature conclusions when you don't have all the pieces of the puzzle, Scorpio. It takes a long time interacting with a person before you get what makes them tick. Refrain from sharing these psychological observations early on. No one likes it when a date degenerates into an attempted free psychotherapy session offered by someone who barely knows them—and who ends up being wrong most of the time. Keep things light in the beginning and trust that the depth you love will form in time if it's meant to.

Scorpios also need to guard against turning their date into a corporate pressure interview. Look, none of us wants to waste each other's time. But sometimes Scorpios can get impatient and ask hard and intense questions way too early about money, kids, marriage, converting religions, family, relocating, etc. What they seem to miss is how the most important question is right in front of them: Can you relax, giggle, and kick back with this person? None of the other stuff matters if that foundation isn't there. There are many people who look good on paper and check all our boxes that we can't even fathom coming home to at the end of the day.

It would be better for Scorpios to ask light questions like "What kind of restaurants do you like?" and "What kinds of activities do you enjoy?" Use the information you gather and do your homework. Circle back and pitch a place for the next date that the food critics are raving about that serves the food they crave. Scorpios possess amazing research skills with a passion for getting to the bottom of things. It's really alluring when Scorpio finds that hidden gem that makes for a lovely evening. And it's a much better outlet for their research skills than amateur psychoanalysis.

SCORPIO LOVERS

It may seem like we've devoted a lot of time to the mistakes that Scorpios make early on in dating, but the truth is that the most common reason Scorpios are single is because they come on too strong too early in dating. But Scorpio's dogged fierceness makes them incredible as long-term partners. They can take the heat that comes with intimacy.

Few signs are better with sex than Scorpio. Everyone enjoys sex. But Scorpios often get it better and more profoundly.

Some Scorpios may experience sexual trauma and feel blocked, but they actually have an incredible capacity to unblock and enjoy sex as adulthood unfolds. This sign responds well to sex therapy, which taps into the flow of the Lethe that we explored in chapter two.

Scorpios will meticulously research the person's body to figure out just what gets them off. And while other folks can get lazy, Scorpios view it as their solemn responsibility to do right by their lover and go full-throttle between the sheets. And not just at the beginning, but throughout the relationship—even after the honeymoon period ends. Scorpios are also masters at make-up sex. They love to show their lover that they still care after a spat by going down on them like there is no tomorrow.

One of the most amazing parts of being truly intimate with a Scorpio is that no story and no subject is off-limits. The way their intensity can be a net negative in early dating turns into a net positive as true intimacy begins to unfold. Other sun signs can subtly discourage the open sharing that makes bonding possible. Scorpios know just what to say after their lover shares a hard part of their story and knows just what to say to remind that person that they don't need to be perfect to make Scorpio happy.

Nothing turns a Scorpio on more than when their partner asks for some help in exorcising their inner demons. All of us have unresolved psychological issues. Whereas other signs get intimidated when things get complex, Scorpios get even more into it and are all-in. Just as we all have our sexual spots that get us off, we also have our emotional sweet spots. Scorpios delight in using all their depth and intensity to craft the most incredible pep talk. They love to inspire their partners to take the next step or the next leap of faith.

Nevertheless, it's important that Scorpios allow their partners to initiate and say, "This is where I need some support." Or, if the partner is not forthcoming, a gentle "How can I support you this week?" can be helpful. The danger for Scorpios is when they start deciding that their close bond means they get to tell someone else how to live their life. Unsolicited feedback is rarely well received, especially when one partner goes for the other's jugular, which Scorpions can do when they sense someone is blocked.

Scorpios need to work with their anger as they endure the humanity of their partners. We are *all* works in progress. And it is human to miss the mark when we aim high.

But Scorpio needs to pause and reflect on why their partner doesn't hit the bull's-eye every time. They may jump to the conclusion that their partner is being a wimp and needs to man up (or woman up). But the truth is more complex. We all wake up in the morning and aspire to be successful, sane, sociable, and loving. What brings us down is our unresolved emotional issues. We err again because there is a hard feeling we are bearing, and what we often need is more support.

Saint Francis de Sales once observed: "Nothing is so strong as gentleness, nothing so gentle as real strength." Now, this paradoxical aphorism may well seem like outdated nonsense to a Scorpio. Don't underestimate the power of the gentle question, and tenderness after a setback. In dentistry, it takes gentleness to remove a cavity. And so, when it comes to helping our partners face the music of their unresolved issues, a soft, light touch can go a long way. Ultimately, Scorpio has to decide whether they care more about dramatic means or dramatic results. If you want to lose your shit on someone, inflict a shame spiral, and watch nothing change, go ahead. Often, gentler, softer dialogues can produce the deeper shifts Scorpio craves.

The ancient myth of the giant scorpion constellation in the sky is actually a love story. And it offers several lessons for Scorpios as they embrace the dance of love. There are many variants but let's tell the story this way:

There was once a good-looking, but conceited hunter named Orion. One day, while wandering through the woods, Orion came upon a naked woman bathing. He immediately turned away out of respect and humility. What he did not realize is that this was not a human woman, but actually the goddess Artemis. Impressed by his respect for her modesty and captivated with his fine skills and good looks, the goddess decided to take Orion as her hunting companion. The two went hunting every day. But Orion eventually made the grave mistake of bragging that he surpassed Artemis's prowess as a hunter. Enraged that a mere mortal would claim greater power than a goddess, Mother Earth decided that Orion had to be punished for his hubris so she sent a giant scorpion,

Scorpio, to kill Orion. Skilled as he was, Orion was no match for Scorpio. The gods then placed Orion and the scorpion as a constellation in the night sky to warn humans of the dangers of big egos.

Scorpios—whatever their gender expression or sexual preference—can often step into the role of Orion in a relationship. They bring much strength, intensity, skill, and sexual desire. What's really key for the success of the relationship is to have a light touch. Looking away from the bathing Artemis is a metaphor for the reward that comes from holding back. The image of two hunters out on a hunting trip together with a bit of friendly competition but always having each other's back might be a powerful archetype for Scorpios to explore. And think of date night as two hunters sitting by the fire, swapping stories and getting ready for their next adventure. Be forewarned: it can all go to hell when Scorpios start acting like they are better than their other half. Don't underestimate how attractive and powerful humility and grace can be!

SCORPIO

at Work

Scorpio can quickly take to the dog-eat-dog environment of the corporate workplace. Many Scorpios have what it takes to fight for their success and climb the ladder. But the challenges come fast as well.

The trouble is that Scorpios can get bogged down in pointless power struggles. They can waste precious time duking it out with another professional when instead they could be pouring all their energy into the next project that will make them a success. If you're a Scorpio and you are reading this advice, this probably isn't the first time you've heard this: Pick your battles and keep your eye on the prize. With that in mind, let's go through the different bombs that can blow up in Scorpio's face and explore how to better maneuver around these mines in the workplace.

SCORPIO VS. EMAIL

For many Scorpios, the inbox can be excruciatingly frustrating. Now, let's be honest—the twenty-first century is rife with folks writing terse words in emails that they wouldn't have the guts to say in person. And there are many little twists of phrase people put in emails that smack of immature passive-aggressive nonsense. Such tactics can drive those born under the sign of the scorpion bonkers. At least once every workday, Scorpios receive an email that completely infuriates them. It takes a bit of work for them to calm themselves down, avoid overreacting, and write poised and professional responses.

Scorpio's colleagues might pick up on their tendency to go ballistic when they get triggered by an email. Scorpio needs to be vigilant and careful about how a nemesis in the workplace may intentionally push their buttons to provoke a reaction and make poor Scorpio look like a maniac. Scorpio, please don't take the bait when you get a message that is clearly "off." Yes, it's hard for you not to respond with something even more vicious when you feel like you've been slighted, and it feels like the agressor is getting away with it if you don't answer back with force and bravado. But sadly, sometimes these messages are actually cleverly laid traps. Most Scorpios early on in their career learn the hard way that whatever you write in an email is just one Forward to your boss away. And their enemies at work might try and use mind games via email to get Scorpios to crack and write something they will regret. When Scorpio claims that the initial email was inflammatory, the boss says that a terse email doesn't warrant that kind of overkill response.

SCORPIO VS. COWORKERS

When a colleague gets under Scorpio's skin, they're often told to "calm down." Scorpio has heard this piece of advice numerous times. But Scorpio misinterprets this to mean "stop fighting." And for a sun sign ruled by Mars, fighting is a big part of life. So let's explore it in a different way. There are many ways to fight back. Let's take a proverb from Sun Tzu's *The Art of War*: "The Supreme Art of War is to subdue the enemy without fighting." What if you forwarded the initial aggravating email to your boss and asked for advice on how to respond? What if you ignored it? There are so many other ways to win without fighting. So instead of telling yourself to calm down, ask yourself: How can I be more strategic? Is there a way to lose the battle but win the war?

Most Scorpios hate meetings with a burning passion. They loathe sitting there and listening to people brainstorm stupid ideas. They despise watching the boss make a fake smile and avoid telling people to their face how silly that idea was. They also hate when people give rationalizations for their mediocrity when pressed on why a project has fallen behind. They resent what they interpret to be the boss giving their colleagues a free pass for missing a target. In truth, the boss is just trying to be diplomatic and regain some momentum. Sometimes, Scorpio can lose their cool at a meeting and launch into a harsh and mean diatribe, creating a super-uncomfortable silence. Bear in mind that if someone else looks bad at a meeting, it is really their problem and their raise that's on the chopping block. But while this may seem logical, Scorpio can struggle to hold back, especially when they feel like the boss is cutting everyone too much slack. And other colleagues start to resent how Scorpio keeps trying to bust their chops with feisty looks or pointed comments. Just remember: you aren't the boss.

SCORPIO VS. DIPLOMACY

Scorpios also have a way of naming the elephant in the room that the boss is diplomatically trying to avoid. Sometimes your boss is going to call a meeting to try to offer the person they are gently calling out a way to save face and get back on track. As Sun Tzu wrote in *The Art of War*, "Build your opponent a golden bridge to retreat across." And Scorpio blows it all up by saying, "Well, we all know that we wouldn't be in this situation if this person hadn't screwed up." When this happens, your coworkers will probably say something like, "You just had to say that, didn't you?" It's true, and everyone was thinking it. But was it necessary? And shouldn't the focus be on moving forward? Scorpios would do well to ponder the words of Winston Churchill, who said: "Diplomacy is the art of telling people to go to hell in such a way that they ask for directions."

Scorpios get way too psychological and intense with their bosses. There is a school of thought out there that believes the way to achieve success is to get inside your boss's head, figure out what makes them tick, and then to ingratiate yourself to him or her as much as possible. And this appeals to the little Freud inside of every Scorpio way too much. But they can get carried away with inventing elaborate fantasies that the little thing they said in the elevator, or that extra line in the email they spent fifteen minutes sweating over, will somehow be the key to the kingdom. And they're just plain wrong when they get carried away with these ideas.

The truth is that most bosses care about results. In most places, there are bottom lines that are as clear as crystal. Are you making money for the company? Are you meeting deadlines? Are you creating excellent work products? Do you keep making the same mistakes or are you adjusting based on the feedback you're getting? Do you arrive to work on time? Do you play games when it comes to vacation time? Sometimes Scorpios can delude themselves into thinking that they don't have to meet these basic targets because they have their boss "figured out" and therefore they can cut corners. But bosses can pick up on this pretty quickly, and they actually hate it when Scorpios try to play them for fools.

SCORPIO VS. DRAMA

Scorpio can be a big gossip at work. Well, maybe "gossip" isn't exactly the right term, since they play detective to try to get everyone else to spill the beans but seldom share much themselves. Similar to their boss dynamics, Scorpios can convince themselves that the workplace is a mystery novel. And that if they learn every colleague's backstory, and read in between all the lines, they will discover the mystical key to success that will catapult them beyond their wildest dreams. This is where Pluto, lord of the underworld, ruling Scorpio can really cause problems. Scorpios can get carried away and invasive with their coworkers, when what they really need to do is just work hard and get the next task at hand done efficiently. Now, of course, many workplaces have interpersonal dimensions, but Scorpio can get way too caught up in the drama. Meanwhile, it's really amazing how many workers in the twenty-first century struggle with basic issues of focus and concentration. It's not as exciting as attempting to manipulate the palace intrigue of your workplace; but if your goal is to set yourself apart, nothing shines brighter than being the hardest worker who knows how to put their nose to the grindstone, avoid getting sidetracked by the drama, and just focus on meeting deadlines and getting projects to the finish line.

Now, all this fascination with secrets and psychology has another very strange effect on Scorpio. They are very aware of just how screwed up everyone is at their job. They can't hold back from prying into their coworkers' life stories and getting involved in the drama. And this means they often know why someone keeps making the same mistake over and over again, and they can become really frustrated and enraged with that colleague. There may be some point to the aphorism that ignorance is bliss—it probably would be better for Scorpio not to know these things about the people they work with. Most Scorpios need to just let other people dig their own graves. How much is that other person's mediocrity affecting you? Do you really need to spend so much time thinking about and analyzing it?

If someone you work with keeps screwing up consistently, and is endangering your shot at success, don't appoint yourself her fixer. Speak to that person's supervisor, because ultimately it's the company's product and reputation that's on the line. Scorpios often don't like to bring things to their boss's attention. They may fear being called a snitch. Or, more likely, it's because they don't know how to broach the conversation without ripping their colleague a new one and coming off too harsh. The key to this is to use soft language that sounds like you are drinking the Kool-Aid. Here's a script: "Shirley, I want to be successful and get these projects completed. I am wondering if you have any feedback on how I could work with Jim more effectively. I've noticed a pattern and I'm curious if you have any advice on how we can resolve this and be more successful." Scorpios find such sugarcoating to be annoying. But the point is to send a subtle hint at the actual issue while simultaneously conveying that you are committed to keeping things positive, professional, and humble. If Scorpios show their stingers too much and come down on a colleague too hard behind their back, even if the observations are true, the supervisor will suspect that Scorpio has personal animus and may discount what's been said, even though it is actually the bitter truth.

Scorpios may resent their bosses for not having "fixed" everyone—although hopefully Scorpio is wise enough to understand that bosses seldom are able to hire the perfect employee. Nor do most people actually seriously listen to the feedback their bosses give them and make changes. People try for a little bit and then slip back into certain patterns. Most bosses are busy trying to put out the biggest fire of the moment, trying to find a way to move the ball forward as human beings make mistakes they have already been gently told about, to keep the peace when folks start to bicker.

THE SCORPIO BOSS

The day that Scorpio starts to supervise people is a rude awakening for all involved. Scorpio discovers just how stubborn most adults are and how all the deep insights that they share can end up feeling like pearls thrown before swine. Scorpios as supervisors can give some of the most intense and powerful performance reviews. They really want to help all their employees become better. But it can be really hard to watch so many employees be unable or unwilling to integrate the feedback they get and put it to work. Scorpios need to remind themselves that not everyone gets promoted for a reason, to stick with the winners, and to reassign or fire someone that isn't working out after they've blown their chances to adjust. The workplace is not the place for taking on people as special charity projects. Save that energy for your family and for when your good friends have bad things happen to them and ask for support and help.

As bosses, Scorpios can, at times, be too hard on the people they supervise. And when you are mean to people, they usually start to be mean right back and resent you. As supervisors, Scorpios need to be able to do the professional equivalent of "kiss and make up." But they can be reluctant to be affectionate toward subordinates until they see the changes they want. The problem is that when you feel like your boss viscerally hates you, it's hard to feel motivated to make the hard changes they've asked you to implement. Instead, you start looking for another job while you are at work and begin to cut corners. Once again, this is another place where a light touch can work wonders.

Overall, Scorpio's formula for success in the workplace boils down to some simple slogans: Don't set off fireworks. Keep the drama to a minimum. Stay laser-focused on the tasks at hand. Don't get bogged down in all the "he-said, she-said" that doesn't matter. Be kind. And remember, we work to live, we don't live to work. Keep your team focused on being successful so that you all can enjoy the abundance you're earning with the people you truly care about.

SCORPIO

in School

S corpios can raise hell at home as toddlers. Parents may well breathe a sigh of relief when it comes time for their little scorpion to head off to preschool or kindergarten.

But the parents also probably hold their breath a bit, because they know a major test is coming for their young Scorpio children. How will they navigate group dynamics in the classroom and on the playground? Will they make new friends? Many parents end up surprised that their Scorpio kid, who can raise such hell at home, can behave at school as the first reports from the teacher come in. But the truth is that little Scorpios may well simply excel at not getting caught by the teacher. Many figure out how to ensure that none of their classmates snitch on them.

And it is here, often in the early school days, that Scorpio children first discover the power of secrecy. They learned how to get kids to guard their own, lest they get caught. It is crucial for every Scorpio to explore what childhood taught them about secrets. Perhaps, in early school years, little scorpions also discovered how to get their classmates to divulge their secrets in a one-on-one moment during recess. And then later on, Scorpio turned this knowledge against them to achieve an agenda. The term "emotional blackmail" might sound too sophisticated for a child. But Scorpio children find ways to engage in psychological warfare to protect themselves or the friends they care about on the schoolyard. The other children quickly learn not to cross the little Scorpio. But they may also decide to gang up on Scorpio to settle the score, which can be very hard for Scorpio to bear—but the bitter truth is that the little scorpions set themselves up for being ganged up on by playing mind games with everyone.

SCORPIO IN ELEMENTARY SCHOOL

In elementary school, Scorpio kids can fight dirtier than necessary. If a classmate says or does something that offends them, they may strike back and hit below the belt. Or do nothing but hold on to a silent grudge that festers until one day Scorpios blow up and retaliate over something that happened ages ago. Parents of Scorpio children can help their child by explaining to them that when someone is off and does something weird, it may not have anything to do with them. Sometimes a person is just having a bad day, didn't sleep well, or is feeling really crushed about a disappointment. It's not first nature for most Scorpio kids to de-escalate. And these kids, quick to take umbrage, have a way of exacerbating instead of resolving conflicts when left to their own devices on the playground.

So much of the tension at school traces back to the deep-seated belief—one that many Scorpios bear—that the way to stay safe is to fight and take on the role of the adversary. As other sections of this book have already outlined, other signs have different theories about how to stay safe. In school, it's similar: Libras wear great outfits and try to master the art of diplomacy. Geminis are constantly trying to master the art of talking. Capricorns just try to be the best student and work harder than everyone else, etc. It can be helpful for parents to remind their Scorpio child that their classmates are not out to get them. However, they should know that if they consistently step on other people's toes, their peers are going to retaliate. And sometimes young Scorpios can fall into a vicious cycle with another classmate, where they both can't stop giving each other a hard time. It can be challenging for the Scorpio child to stop fighting and break out of that loop.

At school, there may be another classmate that becomes the nemesis of the Scorpio child. Little ones born in the sign of the scorpion can experience intense envy if another classmate is smarter, taller, stronger, or more desirable than they are. While most of us experience a peer who far excels us in some way as children, casting that person as an enemy to be vanquished is the scorpionic way of coping. Scorpio children need to be constantly reminded of the abundance of this world. Many adults need this reminder, too. There is enough space for multiple talented people to all be successful. Scorpios can squander their time and energy in elaborate schemes to sabotage their so-called enemies in the schoolyard instead of focusing on doing their homework and playing around with other kids with whom they share interests. Other Scorpios seem less aggressive on the outside, but smolder quietly with resentment and then strike at an opportune time. They waste a lot of mental time nursing their grudges.

SCORPIO IN MIDDLE SCHOOL

The transition from elementary school to middle school is hard for many Scorpios. Puberty is not easy for any sun sign. But it is particularly challenging for Scorpios, because sexual desire plays such a long and important role in their lives. After all, their sun is ruled by Mars, which rules, among many things, sexual desire and lust. In addition, among many medical astrologers, there is the consistent observation that Scorpio energy corresponds to the genitals. Scorpios are more receptive, and note small changes more, than their peers. And they may compare their sexual development to their peers, worrying that they don't measure up. Locker-room experiences can be particularly painful for Scorpios. They can become so frightened when they observe their peers developing. Parents can try to help by reminding their children gently that teens develop at different paces. But very often, Scorpio chooses not to share the most difficult moments with their parents. One of the best things that a parent can do is to allow space for a best friend to step in and help with these issues. Many Scorpios latch onto a friend that can help them explore all this intensity, someone who they feel has their back instead of competing with them or trying to bring them down.

Most Scorpios have a hard time in middle school as their first serious crushes develop. Often, Scorpio feels attracted to another classmate but discovers the feelings aren't reciprocal. Or perhaps Scorpio gets the other end of the stick. Maybe another classmate crushes on them but they aren't interested and struggle with how to stop the advances and get the other kid to move on. Other Scorpios do start to date in that strange way in which middle schoolers imitate adult rituals. But very often they are taken aback by the intensity of everyone else's interest in the romance. They also can become disoriented as the dynamics with the person they are dating shift from the pink cloud of shared fascination to decisions about how far they are going to go sexually.

Now, of course, almost all middle schoolers experience the awkwardness of first crushes. But for Scorpios, these experiences leave a deeper impression, and it might be harder for them to move on. And Scorpio teens can be quick to decide that all future romantic situations are going to unfold just like the first one. They may shut down, worry that they are defective and unlovable, or never forgive the other person for their first disappointment.

As middle school unfolds, Scorpio's jealousy triggers abound. They may resent the rich kid who shows up in fancy clothes. They may envy the classmate who is more handsome or beautiful than they are. They may begrudge the kid who gets better grades. What can be painful about middle school is that childhood is over, and life becomes more complicated. The natural advantages that certain individuals possess begin to show up. This may be hard for some readers to stomach, but privilege is real. And Scorpios can take it very hard when they start to get hip to the fact that some of their peers benefit from advantages they don't.

As middle school goes on, the evening homework pile gets taller, but the social media accounts also start to come online. Online bullying is a black hole that Scorpios can easily get trapped in. As they become aware of the advantages their classmates have, they also become aware of their weaknesses. And they try to craft an attack that can pierce through these chinks in the armor. It's an epic waste of time, but Scorpios are drawn to this verbal sparring from a safe distance like a moth to a flame. Parents will have their work cut out for them, trying to persuade their little Scorpio that they will be happier and more fulfilled in life if they can focus on building themselves up rather than trying to rip other people down.

SCORPIO IN HIGH SCHOOL

High school draws Scorpios out in a very different way than elementary or middle school. Indeed, parents will probably notice sudden shifts and changes in their teen that seem to come from nowhere. In high school, what dawns on many Scorpios is that it's going to be competitive to get into college. There may be an inkling of a career they want to pursue, and they will quickly discover that they are going to have to get good grades and score better than others on tests to get there. For many Scorpios, the recognition of this competition flicks a switch on inside them. And suddenly, they discover a new, almost-obsessive focus.

Not all Scorpios handle this competitive reality well. Some become stricken with panic and fear that they won't measure up. Others perform obsessive research on what they are trying to master and absorb nonsense from some of the stranger corners of the Internet. They can get overwhelmed, decide they don't want to play the game, and latch on to conspiracy theories that the world is about to go to hell in a handbasket anyway, so what is the point in trying to be successful? Parents will need to work with their Scorpio teens during the high school years to help them cope with the reality of competition.

High school is also a time when psychology first begins to be something that most Scorpios can attune to and appreciate. They are going to become aware of the neuroses of their classmates, their friends, their parents, and their teachers. And it's going to be very dispiriting as they come to realize how "screwed up" everyone is. As is often the case, they may decide to go on the offensive. There might be a teacher that they try to embarrass in class, hoping to prove to everyone that they aren't doing their job. There may be a friend they get fed up with and decide to call out in brutal fashion. Or they may turn on their parents and use everything they've ever learned about them against them in biting, mean attacks. And then Scorpio teens often discover that other people can fight back and say equally vicious things to them about the shortcomings that they are working on. There might be a danger of stirring up more drama than necessary and engaging in a tit-for-tat that doesn't actually help anyone heal.

Many Scorpios have intense experiences with sex and dating during high school. Very often, what comes up for them are issues of control. They may try to control their significant other. Or they may attract someone who tries to control them. Teenagers have a difficult time negotiating when they want to do different things. Other sun signs have an easier time compromising and reaching a truce that both can live with. But Scorpio doesn't like to feel weak and takes it very personally when that other person doesn't want to cater to their every whim and go along with every plan they hatch. Many Scorpios don't understand how off-putting it can be to try and control someone like this.

Scorpios do not deal well with their senior year of high school. They are often taken aback by who "wins" and who "loses" when it comes to getting into or rejected from first-choice colleges. Very often, that quieter kid who just sort of steered clear of Scorpio's antics and focused on their work does really well. And the kid that Scorpio admired for their skill at psychological warfare doesn't. It sounds trite to talk about reaping what you sow. But the truth is that hard work eventually pays off. And if Scorpio isn't able to learn this lesson soon enough, they may find themselves entering the next phase of life with the realization that they spent too much time getting bogged down in high-school drama and not enough on what will actually position them for success in the long term.

SCORPIO

in Daily Life

Scorpios have a certain routine they love to stick to. And they are convinced that these habits are the source of all their strength, power, and prowess in this world. Truth be told, sometimes Scorpios thrive in spite of—not because of—their daily routines. Adults born in the sign of the scorpion can cling to some outdated habits that might have worked ten years ago. But there is something so adamant about Scorpios. They made a promise to themselves. As one of the most persistent signs in the zodiac, sometimes they can't distinguish between when tenacity helps and when obstinate stubbornness works against them. Life evolves, circumstances change, and the beat goes on. It behooves us all to reexamine our patterns and experiment to see if a new daily ritual can help us to be sharper at work and happier with friends and family.

SCORPIO MORNING

So let's start with the morning. Most Scorpios wake up too early and head to bed too late. They burn the candle at both ends too often and don't allow themselves enough sleep. This warlike spirit can lead them to desire to take a day by storm and try to pack too much in. Mars is the sign's ruler, and this war god can make Scorpios feel that there are many little battles they need to duke out before the day is done. But truth be told, those born in the sign of the scorpion can invent a false sense of urgency around some tasks because they feel royally pissed about them. They can't stand not doing anything about a particular thing that aggravates them. Maybe a subordinate messed up in a small way. Maybe it's a mistake on their bill from the phone or power company. Waiting feels like letting it fester. And this leads them to take on too much, some days.

Yes, there is that anti-procrastination slogan "Don't put off until tomorrow what you can do today." But there is another slogan that Scorpios might find useful: "Don't try to function on 5 hours of sleep for several days in a row." Sleep deprivation makes us less efficient at tasks and more likely to make mistakes that cost us time and money. Not getting enough sleep also makes us emotionally volatile and can lead us to create drama that ends up wasting more precious time. Scorpios may be surprised by how much more effectively they work when they get more sleep.

Imagine you're a warrior heading to battle. Would you leave the barracks grouchy, woozy, and hungry? It sounds silly for soldiers to rob themselves of sleep and food when they are about to put their lives on the line. But many Scorpios do just that when they cut corners on self-care because there is some fight that can't wait. And they put their livelihoods at risk more than they think, because—as every boss knows—no one is indispensable.

Scorpios love coffee. And they might lean on it a little too much as they go about trying to function on less sleep than is healthy. Many Scorpios might drink too much coffee and eat too small a breakfast. It sounds old-fashioned to extol the values of a real breakfast, but there's a reason why farmers take it so seriously. The key to having sustained energy throughout the day is to balance protein, fat, and carbs in the morning. Many Scorpios may be trying to lose weight by cutting corners with breakfast. But as many nutritionists will advise you, the place to cut calories is at the end of the day with a small dinner. Coffee can also make any of us irritable and jumpy. And the caffeine crash when breakfast is too small is real.

The challenge here is that Scorpios might not think being irritable from eating a substandard breakfast is a problem. If someone pisses them off and an interaction gets nasty, that's their problem, right?

When Scorpio arrives at work in the morning, they are going to have to swallow some grudges. Despite being enraged that someone won't do them a solid because of how irritable and annoying they've been, they are very likely to have a shitlist of people they wish to punish. Now, it's totally valid to have hard feelings about how some people have mistreated us. But success is about setting aside those feelings, letting go, and prioritizing what the team needs done and what our boss needs to see some movement on. No one is asking you to be best friends with the people you work with. But why hold yourself back from being successful to prove a point to someone who probably doesn't care?

SCORPIO MIDDAY

Lunch breaks are often underestimated by Scorpios. Why take a real lunch when there's so much work to do? Well, part of what lunch does that's so incredible is that after relaxing for an hour, it's easier to get work done in the afternoon. Maybe there's a meeting or a call that is going to be annoying as hell, and we keep putting it off. Perhaps we have to clean up someone else's mess on a project and have been postponing it for a few days. The fact is, that emotional hit is going to be easier to withstand if we've taken the time to step away and recharge.

When the weather is nice, consider eating in a park. Nature works wonders, especially if there is a pool of water or a fountain that will speak to the subconscious of this water sign. And after even just thirty minutes outside with trees and sun, we can often return to our desks with a sharper focus, ready to take the afternoon work session by storm. It may not be a combative strategy, but sometimes it's good for Scorpio to just relax and release tension. It's similar to how sailors are more effective on the ship after some shore leave. If there is a colleague you get along with, maybe try to plan to get lunch together on a slower day. Don't make it anything too serious—just laugh and giggle over workplace politics as only colleagues can do.

In the afternoon, the pace starts to drop off as mental fatigue kicks in. Sometimes Scorpio can misjudge what's an appropriate conversation to initiate with colleagues in the late afternoon or early evening. Ask yourself: Is it essential to bring this up now? Or would it be better to check in about it in the morning, when everyone has fresh eyes? It's important here to consider the growing body of evidence for a phenomenon known as "decision fatigue." To summarize, adults can only make so many decisions per day. And toward the end of the day, they often reach their limit and either can't decide or have to force themselves to make an important decision, in which they can end up making a choice they'll come to regret. So it's crucial here for Scorpio to focus on closing out and not trying to persuade anyone about their big new idea at 4:57 P.M.

Scorpios also need to be realistic about their own mental limits and their own workflow. Sometimes those born under the sign of the scorpion can overestimate their willpower. Plan to do the hardest tasks in the morning as much as you can and leave the easy stuff for the afternoon. And if you must challenge a colleague to get the result your boss needs, try to do it diplomatically in the morning, when there is a greater chance of it being well received. If this exchange provokes aggression, you'll be able to handle it more reasonably if you're mentally prepared. Even when you're right, people can be unpleasant and unprofessional, and it's easier to take the high road in the morning.

SCORPIO EVENING

The evening brings its own opportunities and temptations for Scorpio. And there are a few different ways this can go.

Most Scorpios need to work on surrounding themselves with amazing friends to chill out with in the evening. It can take work to cultivate new friends as an adult, but it's worth the investment. And really, what it takes is a willingness to schedule with other adults who are just as busy as you are. Scorpios can be loyal to a fault and can try and stick by the same lifelong friends, but sometimes people change as they grow older, and they are no longer healthy to be around. It's crucial to cut our losses and move on when a friendship is no longer beneficial. We may also lose friends in more direct ways: they move away from us, have kids, go to grad school, or some other life shift draws them away from us. Or there is a silly misunderstanding, and you part ways.

Abandonment can be hard, and it's a valid feeling that someone is irreplaceable. But sometimes, when social situations become too tough, Scorpios decide to just go home to watch TV and stare at their phones instead of doing the work and facing the difficult feelings. And let's be honest—an active social media presence isn't the same thing as having a stable of real friends to meet with a few nights a week to enjoy some drinks, kick back, and laugh with. It's a brutal feeling to feel lonely at home and hope that someone will like and comment on a post you just wrote.

Scorpios can benefit immensely from a hobby. It can give them a great way to unwind and relax when they need to recharge on their own. Conversely, it's also a great way to meet people. Don't be one of those Scorpios who works all day with a mean attitude and then comes home and broods. If you're into art, go check out an art opening. If you're into sports, head to a game and make friends with other fans. Join a book club, go hiking, join a sports team, sing in a choir. If you're single, one of the best ways to meet a quality person is to find someone with similar interests at an event. If you're in a relationship, one of the best ways to keep the fire burning is to balance joint mutual interests while also allowing space to develop separate interests when the two of you need a break from each other.

Unwinding after a long day is serious business, Scorpio. And as alluring and expansive as the Netflix offerings are, it pays dividends to invest in cultivating a rich social life and exploring your hobbies. Scorpios can bring a lot of depth to the conversations they carry on with friends. And it will help them to become less morose and vindictive when they can be friends with people they can laugh with at night to release the day's cares.

Now, when it comes to falling asleep, it can be tricky for Scorpio. Sometimes the last thing they do before bed is stay up late watching TV—they tend to enjoy shows that are all about power plays, like *House of Cards*, when really what they need to do is go to bed a little earlier.

Although every sun sign can benefit from dream-work, I would argue that Scorpios could benefit the most from it out of any sign in the zodiac. One reason is that with the modern insight that the planet Pluto rules over Scorpio, it makes sense that many Scorpios have a knack for psychology. And it predisposes them to be intrepid decoders of their own dreams, and to be open to exploring their deeper meanings. Many Scorpios feel a hunger for insight and inspiration. But instead of staying up late and trying to get it from TV, experiment with discovering your own inner world. Often, dreams and the process of trying to unravel them like a riddle can be a galvanizing process that ushers in its own breakthroughs. Try mugwort teas and other herbal remedies that can help you dream more vividly. Dream recall is like any other mental task. With focus, it becomes easier and more clear. This is part of the energetic connection Scorpios can build with the river Lethe (see chapter two). There is a profound ability to let go and release. With practice, going to sleep will feel like going to the movies.

8

SCORPIO
in the World

S corpios are some of the most famous, powerful, rich, and glamorous people in the world. The funny thing is that you might not realize just how many celebrities whose stories you already know are actually Scorpios.

And while no one is claiming that all these individuals are identical or even superficially similar, it is really uncanny the way that each life story weaves together Scorpio symbols and themes so richly. There are many ways to resonate with this material.

SCORPIO ON THE SCREEN

Sex appeal is something all movie stars wish they had as much as Scorpio stars. Those born under the sign of the scorpion are in a league of their own. It's really fascinating to observe how each Hollywood star brings out Scorpio themes in their work.

Leonardo DiCaprio (November 11, 1974) set the modern standard with his portrayal of Romeo in 1996's *Romeo + Juliet*. It takes a Scorpio to pull off lust and desire that well. The following year, he outdid himself as Jack in the 1997 blockbuster. *Titanic,* which at the time was the highest-grossing film ever. The sexual intrigue was full-on as he drew Kate Winslet in the nude and then got frisky in a Model T. He was a formidable gangster in 2002's *Gangs of New York.* And since the '90s, he's taken on roles in several Martin Scorsese projects where scorpionic questions of power keep bubbling up.

Jodie Foster's (November 19, 1962) breakthrough moment came early at fourteen, when she portrayed a child prostitute in *Taxi Driver* (1976). That might be the most Scorpio role a teenage actor could take on—and she garnered an Oscar nomination for best supporting actress for it, becoming one of the youngest Oscar nominees of all time. Her work continues to send her to the underworlds of human experience that arguably only a Scorpio can handle. She won her first Oscar for a gut-wrenching role as a rape survivor in *The Accused* (1988). She won her second Oscar portraying an FBI trainee interviewing a serial killer in *Silence of the Lambs* (1993). And like a Scorpio, she kept the secret of her identity as a lesbian for many years and didn't publicly acknowledge it until 2007, giving a somewhat opaque speech about coming out at the 2013 Golden Globes.

Julia Roberts (November 28, 1967) also glows with the kind of intense sex appeal that only a Scorpio can carry. Julia portrayed an escort in *Pretty Woman* (1990) to critical acclaim and commercial success. She won a Golden Globe for the role, and the film notched the highest number of ticket sales ever for a romantic comedy in the U.S. Her glamor and sex appeal has been legendary in many films.

But she wouldn't be a Scorpio unless she was also a fighter. She played an environmental lawyer leading a class-action lawsuit for victims of a polluting power company in *Erin Brockovich* (2000). She won the Oscar for Best Actress that year.

For many years in the 1990s and early 2000s, she was the highest-paid actress in the world. In 2000, she earned $20 million for *Erin Brockovich*. In 2003, she received $25 million for the film *Mona Lisa Smile*. She reportedly proved to be a formidable salary negotiator, as only a Scorpio could be.

SCORPIO IN THE ARTS

In the arts and music, Scorpios are some of the most out-landish performers and provocateurs.

Björk Guðmundsdóttir (November 21, 1965) is one of the few avant-garde musicians who has achieved commercial success. She mixes numerous styles of music and has mesmerized many fans with her unique Icelandic pronunciation and flare for outlandish fashion. She once even famously donned a swan dress while attending the Academy Awards in 2001. In oh-so-Scorpio fashion, she notoriously lost it on a reporter in 1996, when she was barraged by paparazzi at the Bangkok International Airport. She lunged at one reporter, Julie Kaufman, and knocked her to the ground. In 2008, she was assailed by a mob of photographers at the Auckland International Airport. Björk tore one photographer's shirt, causing him to fall to the ground. In 1996, a crazed fan, Ricardo López, sent a bomb in the mail to Björk's London home. The metropolitan police discovered the bomb before it was delivered. López, meanwhile, put on Björk's music and recorded a video of himself committing suicide. He confessed that he aspired to meet Björk in heaven. Björk's public comments to this weird incident are so scorpionic: "I make music, but in other terms, you know, people shouldn't take me too literally and get involved in my personal life." Like a true Scorpio, she wanted to remind everyone of her right to privacy and secrets.

Pablo Picasso (October 25, 1881) redefined what modern art could be with his brand of cubism. He also went through many other phases—his blue phase, his rose phase, and his stained-glass phase, among others. Like a true Scorpio, he kept letting go of what he'd once done and transforming into something new with the flow of the Lethe. And then of course, there was Picasso's notorious sex drive and tendency toward womanizing. One of his most famous paintings at the Museum of Modern Art, *Les Demoiselles d'Avignon* (1907), depicts five nude women in a brothel. It was shocking for its time to portray prostitution on such a monumental scale.

SCORPIO IN POLITICS

In politics, we've watched Scorpios take center stage, challenging and surprising us.

Hillary Clinton (October 26, 1947) is one of the most quintessential Scorpios to have ever come into American politics. So many threads in her life scream Scorpio that it could be its own book. One aspect is her penchant for intense one-liners and her tendency to go for the jugular. During Bill Clinton's 1992 presidential campaign, she made an oh-so-Scorpio remark when asked about her choice to have a career: "I suppose I could have stayed home and baked cookies and had teas, but what I decided to do was to fulfill my profession." Many housewives took umbrage and felt demeaned. Others felt challenged by her ambition. But she was unapologetic, and she dared the entire country to get used to a First Lady who was also a professional.

During her time in the Clinton White House, Hillary had an office in the West Wing, which was unusual for a First Lady. She took on health care and other major policy projects and acted more as an adviser to the president. She did all this in spite of major criticism.

When Hillary moved to the senate in 2000, she was instrumental in setting up a "war room" that Democratic senators could use to track the media and messaging. She also sat on the Armed Services Committee for several years. You can't take Scorpios away from war. And during both her campaigns for president, she was often heralded as a fighter. When Donald Trump was asked to compliment her in a debate in 2016, he even praised her as a fighter.

And of course, she wouldn't be a Scorpio without sexual intrigue. Hillary's choice to stay married to Bill Clinton despite his numerous infidelities has garnered a lot of speculation. Some accuse her of being power-hungry. Those that actually know her in real life—or bother to read her biography—know about the deep love she has for Bill Clinton and about the hard choices she's made regarding forgiveness, letting go, and opening a new chapter in her marriage. Can we get more Scorpio?

When we look at the royal family of Great Britain, Prince Charles (November 14, 1948) epitomizes many Scorpio traits. The love triangle between Prince Charles, Princess Diana, and Camilla Parker Bowles drew massive attention in the 1980s and 1990s. It is a story of secrets, intrigue, and desire. And it's so Scorpio, because Charles has basically stuck with Camilla his entire life—the outdated norms of the British monarchy be damned. Charles and Camilla met at a party in 1971. The story goes that Camilla, knowing about some skeletons in the family closet, cracked this cheeky joke: "My great-grandmother was the mistress of your great-great-grandfather. I feel we have something in common." Charles's Scorpio heart melted right there with this combo of sexual intrigue and family secrets. And he never let go. In 1992, a secretly recorded phone call leaked that Charles satirically aspires to be reincarnated as Camilla's knickers or tampon. When Diana confronted Charles about his infidelity, he responded, "Well, I refuse to be the only Prince of Wales who never had a mistress." When it comes to one-liners that go for the jugular, Prince Charles exemplifies Scorpio. As Diana famously said to an interviewer in 1995, "Well there were three of us in this marriage, so it was a bit crowded." Only a Scorpio could pull off this level of sexual intrigue.

SCORPIO IN SCIENCE AND TECHNOLOGY

In technology, Bill Gates (November 28, 1955) is one of the richest men in the world, one of only three billionaires with a net worth north of $100 billion. He earned his fortune as the CEO and chairman for many years of Microsoft. And of course, any company being led by a Scorpio would be overly aggressive—in this case, Microsoft ran into trouble for violating competition laws. Gates was instrumental in developing the personal computer—and the oh-so-Scorpio idea that you can stash your personal secrets in its memory banks.

In science, Marie Curie (November 7, 1867) is in a league of her own. She coined the term "radioactivity" through her groundbreaking research. She was the first woman to win a Nobel Prize and is the only person to have ever won a Nobel in both chemistry and physics. She was relentless in her desire to better understand and one day harness the energy radioactive materials emit. Her dogged pursuit of revealing the mysteries of science is a total Scorpio trait. Curie once remarked, "Nothing in life is to be feared, it is only to be understood. Now is the time to understand more, so that we may fear less." Now that's a Scorpio passionate about the power of the truth. Albert Einstein once remarked that Curie was the only person he knew who was incorruptible in the face of fame. She lived modestly her entire life, giving away most of the money she earned from prizes to advance the various research projects she endorsed. She refused to patent and profit from the radium she discovered, so that her research could be more widely disseminated and scientific progress would not be impeded. She truly took a vow to do everything possible for science.

CURRENT SCORPIOS

Let's give the last word to Lorde (November 7, 1996), the young singer from New Zealand. She explores her Scorpio intensity in a different but equally potent manner.

In 2013, her hit song "Royals" hit #1 on Billboard's Hot 100 list. At sixteen years old, she was the youngest artist to snag the top slot since Tiffany in 1987. She went on to win two Grammy awards. But when you read the lyrics to the song "Royals," they just drip with scorpionic themes.

It's a powerful song about inventing your own meaning, letting go of the petty status symbols, and focusing on creating your own dream world with someone. It is dripping with scorpionic themes such as blood, violence, and luxury . . . but ultimately what comes through is the pursuit of personal truth. Lorde is right: there is a different kind of buzz—when you are in touch with it makes you truly happy for a moment.

In reading the lives of the rich and famous Scorpios, it can be easy to fall into the trap of feeling there must be something defective if you aren't famous too. But the common pattern is that all these Scorpios committed 100% to who they were in a dogged, persistent way. Even Charles stuck with Camilla in a strange way and eventually married the woman he always wanted to. Scorpios' success grew from that commitment. The vow—and the flow of the river Styx—is a deep part of Scorpio as a fixed water sign. Scorpio, aspire to commit to being yourself with the same tenacity as these remarkable individuals. Even if you don't rise to fame and notoriety, you can be like Lorde and find joy and live that fantasy.

CONCLUSION

The conclusion to this book is not going to be some long-winded riff on being less intense. Because no matter what happens, individuals born under the sign of the scorpion are going to be intense.

My parting words to Scorpio are this—cultivate a wicked sense of humor.

Laugh at the wild adventures of your childhood and your school years. Don't be too hard on yourself. You were still discovering that special spark inside of you. And growing into your scorpion energy is a contact sport.

As adulthood unfolds, find ways to broach the difficult subjects that keep coming up with wit, warmth, and good-hearted humor. Warmth can be very underestimated, but with a bit of kindness it will serve you well when you have to wade into the chilly waters of underworld rivers as often as you do in your life. And when you do have to, as much as possible steer toward Lethe and the art of letting go.

If you're a parent, and your child is pushing at your limits to the point where you know you have to say something, why not crack a joke as the first warning shot? Sometimes kids learn more when they giggle, but they'll still know you mean business.

In love, use everything your deep Scorpio mind can discover about your date to make them laugh. It will make the romance more fun. And as you lean into commitment, remember—doesn't everyone want to be with someone who can make them laugh? Laughter helps to balance out the moments of inevitable tension.

At work, look at a comic or a political cartoon every day. Delight in knowing what kinds of jokes your colleagues will enjoy around the watercooler. Use your Scorpio intuition to divine what will amuse your coworkers as opposed to what will destroy them. And above all, focus on just doing the best work you can do. Laugh off most of the drama instead of getting sucked into it.

In daily routines, giggle at how attached you can become to stuff that's no longer serving you. Isn't it ironic that you often call out other people on their bad habits while you persist with your own? When you're implementing and integrating a new routine and feeling sort of crazy, watch some funny clips on YouTube. Stepping back from your current obsessions works wonders.

As you look out at the world, don't waste your time comparing yourself to the rich and famous. Focus on being completely *you*. Or, as Oscar Wilde once quipped, "Be yourself; everyone else is already taken." Party with your friends late and laugh heartily. Work hard on your projects and then crack some jokes and let go. Giggle at yourself as if you wish you had rich-and-famous-people problems. Money, success, fame, and glamour don't count for much if you don't understand the flow of your own underworld rivers.

Why get bogged down in the drama of life when it could be a comedy instead?

INDEX

SCORPIO

ABOUT THE AUTHOR

DANNY LARKIN is the President of the Association for Young Astrologers. He has studied Hellenistic Astrology with Demetra George and Chris Brennan. In 2019, he toured ancient ruins in Greece with Demetra George. He studied modern and psychological astrology with Liz Greene and the Faculty of Astrology Studies in the UK. Stateside, he studied with Meira Epstein, Rob Hand, John Marchesella, and Annabel Gat. He is certified as the first level by the National Council for Geocosmic Research and is pursuing more advanced certifications.

In 2007, he graduated Magna Cum Laude from Fordham University, earning a Bachelor's with special honors in Art History. He studied broadly, including courses on Ancient Greek art, temple architecture, and pagan religion.

Danny lives and works in New York City. He meets with clients as an astrologer, writes art criticism professionally, and shakes a mean cocktail at his home bar.